D1087882

Brush With Greatness

Vincent van Gogh

Michael DeMocker

PURPLE TOAD
PUBLISHING

Printing   1   2   3   4   5   6   7   8   9

Goya
Leonardo da Vinci
Michelangelo
Monet
Van Gogh

Publisher's Cataloging-in-Publication Data
DeMocker, Michael.
    Van Gogh / written by Michael DeMocker.
        p. cm.
Includes bibliographic references, glossary, and index.
ISBN 9781624691997
1. Gogh, Vincent van, 1820-1888 — Juvenile literature. 2. Painters — Netherlands — Biography — Juvenile literature. I. Series: Brush with greatness.
 ND653.G7 2017
 759.92

Library of Congress Control Number: 2016937173

eBook ISBN: 9781624692000

ABOUT THE AUTHOR: Despite being a dashingly handsome, globe-trotting, award-winning photojournalist and travel writer based in New Orleans, Michael DeMocker is, in truth, really quite dull, a terrible dancer, and a frequent source of embarrassment to his wife, son, and three dogs. Despite being Dutch like Van Gogh, he can't even paint a wall without causing a huge mess.

Contents

Cottage and Woman with Goat, 1885

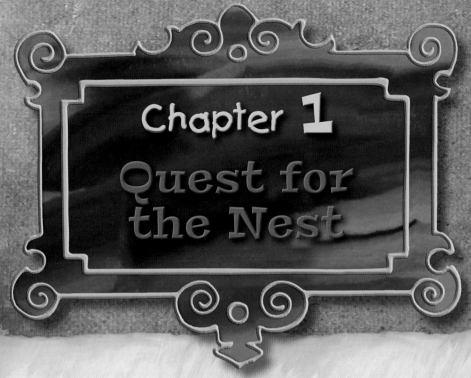

Chapter 1
Quest for the Nest

My name is Peter DeGroot, and I am up a tree. How'd I get here? Let me explain.

In 1885, I was 11 years old and living in a small cottage in the Netherlands with my family. We didn't have very much money, and life was hard.

But a couple years earlier, an artist had moved to town! His name was Vincent van Gogh **(VIN-sent van-GOH)**. Although I didn't know, he would become one of the greatest artists ever.

Van Gogh had come to our part of the world to try his hand at art. He liked to paint pictures of our cottage, which was strange because it wasn't a very nice house. Even though he didn't grow up poor, van Gogh wore ragged clothes and a straw hat.

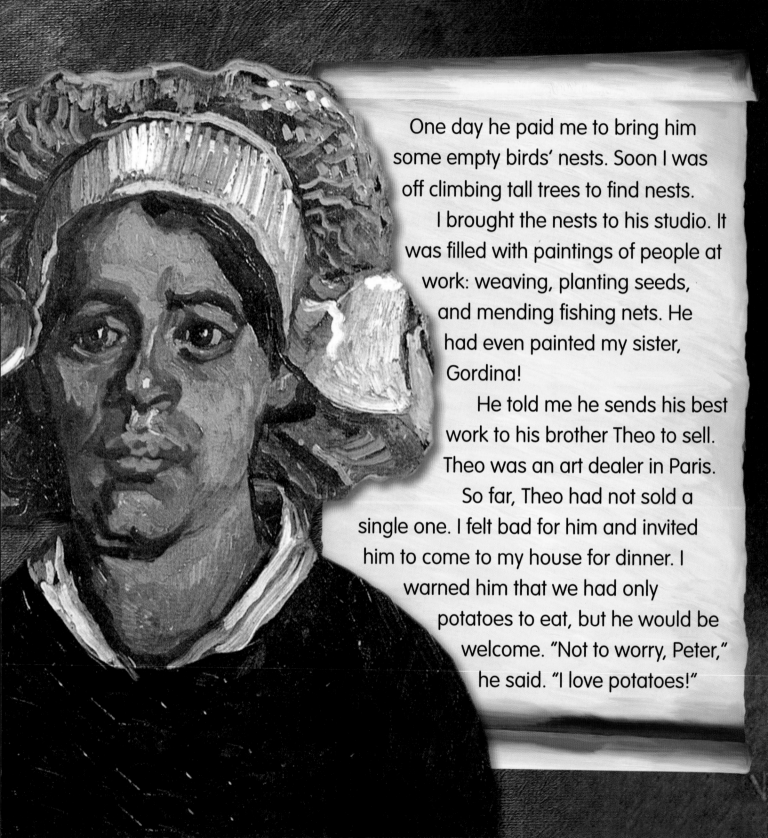

One day he paid me to bring him some empty birds' nests. Soon I was off climbing tall trees to find nests.

I brought the nests to his studio. It was filled with paintings of people at work: weaving, planting seeds, and mending fishing nets. He had even painted my sister, Gordina!

He told me he sends his best work to his brother Theo to sell. Theo was an art dealer in Paris. So far, Theo had not sold a single one. I felt bad for him and invited him to come to my house for dinner. I warned him that we had only potatoes to eat, but he would be welcome. "Not to worry, Peter," he said. "I love potatoes!"

Head of a Peasant Woman with White Cap and *Still Life with Three Birds Nests*, both 1885

Chapter 2
My Family's Famous Dinner

A few weeks later, as I was bringing him more nests, he saw me and yelled, "Peter, get in here! You must see this!"

He led me to an easel, and there was a painting of my family at the dinner table! He truly captured our life at home, except our heads were shaped a little strange.

"I think this is my first masterpiece! I call it *The Potato Eaters*," the artist exclaimed.

Van Gogh must have done 200 paintings during those months. Many were of the peasant people he had grown to love.

He'd always send them off to Paris, but Theo still had no luck selling any. Theo worried about the dark colors he used. They were not as colorful as the paintings being sold in Paris.

Miners' Wives Carrying Sacks of Coal, 1882

One day van Gogh told me it was time for him to move on. He was headed to a place called Antwerp. There he would study the use of color he saw in the museum's paintings. We said goodbye, but he promised he would write to me.

Bridges Across the Seine at Asnières (SEN at an-YAIR), 1887

Months later, I got a letter from Paris!

"Come to Paris, Peter," van Gogh wrote. "I need an assistant. Theo will pay you. It will be a great adventure!"

And before you could say *no more potatoes*, I was on a train heading for the most exciting city in the world.

Once there, I saw that van Gogh had thrown himself into his art. He studied the great painters Henri de Toulouse Lautrec **(on-REE day too-LOOS la-TREK)**, Edgar Degas **(ED-gar day-GAH)**, and Claude Monet **(clawd moh-NAY)**.

His style became brighter and more colorful. He used vibrant yellows, blues, and bright oranges. He painted street scenes, portraits of fellow artists, and still lifes of books and fruit.

I helped him stretch canvasses to paint, and even cooked his meals. He often went days without eating and started to weaken.

Vincent grew cranky, having done 200 more paintings without Theo being able to sell a single one.

My master started painting many pictures of himself. He looked sad in them. Something had to change. So, in 1888, he packed up his paints (and me) and moved to the South of France.

On the Outskirts of Paris, 1887

Sower with a Setting Sun, Arles, and Portrait of Camille Roulin, 1888

Chapter 4
Painting Dreams

We moved into a bright yellow house in Arles **(ARR-el)**, near Paris. His friend, the famous painter Paul Gauguin **(goh-GAN)**, moved in, and soon van Gogh was painting with new energy. Every day we would hike out to the countryside, where he would create bright and colorful paintings of haystacks or sunflowers or wheat fields.

I made friends with a postman's son named Camille Roulin **(kah-MEEL roo-LIN)**. He would sometimes come with us on our painting expeditions. Van Gogh painted his portrait, too. In fact, van Gogh painted everybody in Camille's family!

Van Gogh's paintings became more like those of the famous painters called Impressionists (im-PRESH-uh-nists). The paintings were more colorful, with swirling, thin brush strokes. They showed the light and weren't exact copies of what the artist saw.

Watching him paint a bridge one day, I asked Vincent how he made such stunning paintings. He thought about it, and replied, "I dream my painting, and then I paint my dream."

As those painted dreams got better and better, he did not sleep or eat enough. People noticed how ill he looked. He argued with his friends. Some people thought his mind wasn't right, but I didn't believe it. He was creating so much beauty.

Café Terrace at Night, 1888

Chapter 5

A Star in the Night

But Vincent wasn't okay. Things got so bad, Vincent went to a hospital for help.

I visited him in the hospital. One night, while looking out the window, he said to me, "Peter, I often think that the night is more alive and more richly colored than the day." And he proved it by painting one of his most famous works, *The Starry Night*, while in the hospital.

The Starry Night, 1889

Vincent continued to paint, but he was not feeling better, even though Theo finally sold one of Vincent's paintings. It was called *The Red Vineyard at Arles*. It was the only painting of van Gogh's that sold during his lifetime.

Self Portrait with Grey Felt Hat, 1887 (above) and The Red Vineyard at Arles, 1888

A few months later, Vincent died. He was just 37 years old. Vincent van Gogh came to be known as one of the greatest artists who ever lived. Though he was a painter for only ten years, he produced more than 2,000 drawings and paintings that showed the beauty of nature and humanity.

Bedroom in Arles, (2nd version), 1889 and *The Church at Auvers-sur-Oise* (OH-vayer-sir-WAHZ), 1890

Sunflowers, (4th version), 1888, Wheatfield with Crows, 1890, and Self Portrait as an Artist, 1888

What happened to me? As a reward for my help, van Gogh left me three paintings. They still hang on my wall to remind me of my brush with greatness.

1853   Vincent van Gogh is born in Groot-Zundert, Holland (The Netherlands), on March 30.

1857   Vincent's brother Theo (Theodorus) is born on May 1. They have three sisters and one other brother.

1869   Vincent van Gogh starts working for an art gallery (Goupil & Cie) in The Hague. His job takes him to London and Paris.

1876   Van Gogh teaches English for a while, and then becomes a preacher in Belgium.

1880   He decides to become a painter. Theo supports him.

1885   He completes *The Potato Eaters*.

1886   He moves to Paris, where he meets Impressionist painters. His style becomes brighter and more colorful. It will become known as Post-Impressionist.

1888   Van Gogh moves to Arles, France, to start an art school. He begins suffering from ill health.

1890   Van Gogh dies on July 29. He is buried at Auvers-sur-Oise.

1882	*Miners' Wives Carrying Sacks of Coal*
1885	*The Cottage*
1885	*The Head of a Peasant Woman*
1885	*The Potato Eaters*
1885	*Still Life with Three Birds Nests*
1887	*In the Café: Agostina Segatori in Le Tambourin*
1887	*L'Italienne*
1887	*Self-Portrait with a Grey Felt Hat*
1888	*Bedroom in Arles*
1888	*Café Terrace at Night*
1888	*Portrait of Camille Roulin*
1888	*Self-Portrait as a Painter*
1888	*Sower with Setting Sun*
1888	*Sunflowers*
1889	*Self-Portrait with a Bandaged Ear and Pipe*
1889	*The Starry Night*
1890	*The Red Vineyard at Arles*
1890	*Country Road in Provence by Night*
1890	*The Church at Auvers-sur-Oise*

Country Road in Provence by Night

Further Reading

Works Consulted

Barber, Barrington. *Through the Eyes of Vincent van Gogh*. London: Arcturus Publishing, 2015.

Charles, Victoria. *Vincent van Gogh by Vincent van Gogh*. New York: Parkstone Press International, 2014.

Howard, Michael. *Van Gogh: His Life and Works in 500 Images*. London: Anness, 2010.

Naifeh, Steven, and Gregory White Smith. *Van Gogh: The Life*. New York: Random House, 2012.

Roddam, George. *This Is van Gogh*. London: Lawrence King Publishing, 2015.

Skea, Ralph. *Vincent's Trees*. New York: Thames & Hudson, 2013.

Van Gogh Museum, accessed May 2015, http://www.vangoghmuseum.com/en

Van Gogh, Vincent. *Ever Yours: The Essential Letters*. Edited by Leo Jansen. New Haven: Yale University Press, 2014.

Van Gogh, Vincent. *The Letters of Vincent Van Gogh*. Edited by Ronald de Leeuw. London: Penguin Classics, 1998.

Further Reading

Howard, Michael. *Van Gogh: His Life and Works in 500 Images*. London: Anness, 2010.

Mayhew, James. *Katie and the Starry Night*. London: Hodder & Stoughton, 2013

Van Gogh, Vincent. *Ever Yours: the Essential Letters*. ed. Leo Jansen. New Haven: Yale University Press, 2014.

brush stroke (BRUHSH STROHK)—The mark a paintbrush leaves with one movement.

canvas (KAN-vus)—A special stretched cloth on which artists paint.

easel (EE-zul)—A stand that holds a canvas while it is being painted.

exhibit (eg-ZIB-it)—A show in which artwork is displayed.

Impressionism (im-PREH-shun-isum)—A colorful style of painting that originated in nineteenth-century France that used swirling, thin brush strokes or dabs of paint that re-create the effect of light.

masterpiece (MASS-tur-peess)—An especially great piece of created work, like a painting or musical composition.

peasant (PEZ-uhnt)—A poor farmer or laborer who works the land.

portrait (POR-trit)—A drawing or painting that features just a person's head and shoulders.

still life (STIL LIFE)—A drawing or painting of an arranged collection of objects that do not move.

studio (STOO-dee-oh)—A bright room in which an artist creates his or her artwork.

PHOTO CREDITS: All pictures—Public Domain. Every measure has been taken to find all copyright holders of material used in this book. In the event any mistakes or omissions have happened within, attempts to correct them will be made in future editions of the book.

Index